Just Like You
And Other Inspirational Christian Poems

By Julie C. Gilbert

Love Science Fiction or Mystery?

Choose your adventure!
Visit: **http://www.juliecgilbert.com/**

For details on getting free stories.

Acknowledgements:

Thanks to Timothy Sparvero for illustrating
Some of the poems.

Table of Contents:

Acknowledgements:
Introduction:
1. Just Like You
2. Pride
3. Strangers in this Land
4. Vision, Advice, Plea
5. My Corner
6. Why Do I Cry?
7. Sweet Dreams are Made
8. Technology
9. Half-Blind
10. Evil Whispers
11. Three Things
12. Two Stories and a Challenge
13. Arms of the Lord
14. Alive in Him
15. Follow Him
16. Battle for You
17. Captive to Indifference
18. Why Do We Cry?
19. The City
20. Steady
21. Take Time
22. Always
23. Christian Life: Not Easy but Worth It
24. For the Enemy
25. Will I Ever?
26. God Most High
27. Glorious Night
28. Puzzle Piece

29. Praise
30. Beautiful Sight
31. Liquid Prayers
32. Believe
33. Higher Calling
34. Life Beyond
35. Moonlight
36. No Time Like the Present
37. Blood and Renewal
38. Grant me Wisdom
39. Trust the Lord
40. Fingerprint of God
41. Shadowed Smiles
42. Snow Softly Fall
43. The Truth Remains
44. Prepare
45. Hand in Hand
46. No Tragedy Quite Like
47. Stronger than Loss
48. Only Way to Peace
49. Hope in Loss
50. Still Praising
51. Powerful Knowledge
52. To the Hurting
53. Worry is a Luxury
54. He Meant You
55. Promise
56. On Limits
57. Make a Difference
58. Who Needs Luck?
59. Heart of Gold
60. Holy Child
61. Unshakeable

62. Yesterday's Prayer
63. Your Eyes Say
64. Sunset
65. Christianese
66. Praise Anew
67. Strangest Dream
68. Holy Spirit Fire
69. Undeserved Cross
70. Perfect Rest
71. Sense of Worth
72. Simple Battle Cry
73. Awaken
74. Rest in Me
75. Catch the Vision
76. One Family
77. Moonshine
78. Come Alive
79. Pride and Joy
80. Standing Still
81. Reflect the One
82. Guiding Light
Thank you for reading:

Introduction:

Dear reader,

This is the second collection of Christian inspirational poetry. If you missed out on the first, check out *Thin Black Road*.

As before, many of the poems are songs. If you're interested in hearing them, you'll have to email me: **Devyaschildren@gmail.com**.

My goal is that everyone who wishes to have a copy receives one. To that end, I give away paperback copies. You can request a copy by email.

Hope you enjoy following my journey through the years.

Sincerely,

Julie C. Gilbert

1. Just Like You

You're my hope. You're my hero.
You know all I am and what I can be.
Take this hard heart and make it like yours.
Holy Father, I need your heart.

You're my heart. You're my hero.
Let my life reflect your love.
Give me eyes to see past walls.
Give me ears to hear heart cries.
Give me hands that heal in your name.
O Holy Father, I want to be just like you.

You're my Father. You're my hero.
May my spirit walk with you.
Train my mind to see the lost ones.
Tune my ears to hear your voice.
May my soul shine with your light.
Dear Holy Father, I want to be just like you.

You're my light. You're my hero.
You know all I am and what I will be.
Take this one soul and make it like yours.
Dear Dad, I want to be just like you.

2. Pride

Though others may not see,
I know the pride in me.
I was singing, "Praise God."
And thinking, "Am I on key?"
I was saying, "God is love!"
But doubting, "Can He truly love me?"
I was confessing, "I'm a sinner."
And thinking, "Hey, I'm not so bad."
And yet forever and ever I am blessed,
For in my God I shall find my rest.
He is faithful to forgive all of my sins
Again and again and again.

3. Strangers in this Land

Once, long ago, God came to Earth.
Once, long ago, Christ died for all.
I believe this in my heart,
And that is why I can say …

I'm but a stranger in this land.
My true home lies elsewhere.
I'll make it there one day,
But for now, there's work to do.

Do you believe that Christ died for you?
Do you believe that you can be saved?
Do you believe that God's for you?
If this is so, then you and I …

We're only strangers in this land.
Our true home lies elsewhere.
We'll make it there one day,
But for now, there's work to do.

There are others in this world.
They need to hear this truth we have.
They need to know about God's grace,
Then, they'll realize that …

They're only strangers in this land.
Their true home lies elsewhere.
They'll make it there one day,
But for now, there's work to do.

4. Vision, Advice, Plea

I had a vision late last night.
You can call me crazy,
But this is my tale:
A Christian stood at the gates of Heaven
And waited as the gatekeeper referenced a book.
Finally, the angel looked up, smiled, and said,
"You're on my list, He's paid the price…welcome
home!"

Now, I craned my neck as far as I could,
And I caught a glimpse of a gaping wound …
A Christian stood at the gates of Heaven,
And he cried his last tears …
Before walking through, he said,
"I am happy to be home,
But I wasn't ready to go home today.
I had so many plans … so many goals …
So many dreams left undreamed."
Then, he vanished into light.

Well, what does that mean?
What can I learn?
I don't have all the answers,
But here are a few random thoughts.

Every Christian should serve the Lord
In every way they possibly can.
For you never really know the future.
One day, you could suddenly find yourself
Watching the gatekeeper search for your name.

He'll find your name and welcome you home.
And you'll shed your last tears.
Before walking through, you'll say,
"I wasn't ready to go home today …"
Then, you'll vanish into light.

Well, what does that mean?
What can I learn?
Here are a few more random thoughts.

Every non-Christian ought to consider this:
There's no better time than the present time
To get things right with the Lord.
He's paid the price; the gift is free.
Won't you reach out and take it?

Now, if you're thinking, "That's nice,
But I don't believe in Heaven or Hell."
All I can say is consider this:
Whether you believe or not, they're there,
You're so much more than flesh and blood!
You have an eternal home somewhere.
Where that home is … Is totally up to you.

Well, if it's a battle, I will fight it.
With God on my side, I cannot fail.
Through all things uncertain in life
This rare truth shines as a beacon
Of hope to all God's own.

5. My Corner

Though plans fail, fade, and change
Peace reigns in my corner,
That quiet place where worry
Used to rule over
Me, now no more.

Time enough slipped by
While I cowered in my corner.
I'll make my plans
Then waste no time reliving
Each moment.

When I'm worn and slowly fading
I'll retreat to my corner
Where chaos cannot follow
There I'll stay and renew
My faith by prayer.

With Christ in me I am perfectly
At peace in my corner,
This quiet place where I worship
Him who rules over
Me, now and ever more.

Julie C. Gilbert

6. Why Do I Cry?

I sit, surrounded by my tears
And wonder why I cry.
Do I cry for the lost of this world?
Do I cry for turmoil and pain?
Do I cry for some catastrophe?
Do I cry for my own little wants?

All of these reasons are correct,
Though they are not all right.
There is much to cry about.
There is much that gets one down.
There is no reason this time.
There is only God, and me, and tears …
Until some thoughts come to me,
And I must smile.
My God died to save the lost.
My God can cure all pain.
My God is rightly in control.
My God is always a source of strength.

7. Sweet Dreams are Made

Sweet dreams may seem to be fantasies,
But sweet dreams are made of more than these.
They soothe away fear and pain.
Sweet dreams may seem mere happy things
That momentarily divert the mind.
Can you feel it?
This world is dying slowly.
Tragedy strikes around us.
Mankind wars to rule.
People die from hate
And suffer under words flung hastily.
Disease claims some, disaster others.
Both quite natural yet so unnatural.
It wasn't meant to be this way.
Choice led to sin,
And the rest is history.
Do not become cold.
Ask God for sweet dreams.
He will take your burdens,
Setting your mind at ease.
Such is the purpose of sweet dreams.

8. Technology

We dream that technology will deliver us.
We dream of an age of wisdom.
We dream yet forget to enjoy this life.
It is possible to talk to three
Thousand people in an hour
And never learn the name of one.
It is possible to buy your heart's desire
Good or evil, from a musty basement,
Hidden away from everyone.
It is possible to spend untold hours
In a virtual world where you
Can pretend to be anyone.
So much for this age of wisdom.
So much for this new religion.
So much for technology.
I'm not saying it's a curse,
But sin twisted this gift into an irresistible idol.
Once again, we'll worship creation,
Forgetting the Creator.
Seeking freedom, power, peace
And not remembering why.
We dream that technology will deliver us.
We dream of an age of wisdom.
We dream yet forget to enjoy this life.

Just Like You

9. Half-Blind

I can see, but I can't see.
My head is playing tricks on me.
It was only two tiny drops,
But now my eyes are quite useless.
What a reminder that I am fragile!
I know it's temporary,
But this is really scary.
Can't even read the words I write.
Dare I trust myself with a car?
No, I am stuck here for a time.
Half-blind, that describes me well.
Half-blind is also a spiritual state.
Many see, but they do not see.
I pray, dear God, open their eyes!

10. Evil Whispers

What will you do?
What will you do
When the evil one comes
To whisper in your ear.
"You don't need to pray today
Didn't you pray yesterday?
What good can prayer do now?
Look at how much you have to do!
What's one more hour?
What's one more minute?
Just put if off for a while ..."

If you hear these thoughts
The best thing to do is pray right away.
What will it do?
It will unburden your heart
And lift your spirits up.
Prayer will lead you to the throne,
Right to the Holy One,
To the only one who can make you smile
Through all pain.
Let Him unburden your heart.

11. Three Things

Are you a slave to apathy?
What you want to do
You can't bring yourself
To care enough to carry out.
There are three things that will set you free
From a deep sense of apathy:
Jesus, Jesus, and more Jesus.

Only God's Son ever led a perfect life.
Only God's Son ever earned the right
To be the faultless sacrifice
To heal our broken world.

Are you a slave to your sin?
What you don't want to do
You can't stop yourself
From craving every day.
There are three things that will set you free
From sin's strong claim over you:
Jesus, Jesus, and more Jesus.

12. Two Stories and a Challenge

Story One: One day, a child asked just this:
"How will the work of the Lord be done?
This world's so big, and there are so many
Lost who need to hear."

This was the answer the child received:
Some will go far to serve the Lord.
Some will go far indeed
To foreign lands to serve the Lord.

Others will stay right here at home.
Others will stay home to serve.
And so, in this way all will hear,
And all work will be done right.

Story Two: One day, an angel asked just this:
"Who will go far to serve the Lord?
Who will go far to foreign lands
To serve the Lord far from home?"

Some answered that in just this way:
"I will go far to serve the Lord.
I will go far to foreign lands
To serve the Lord where need may rise."

Then, the angel asked just this:
"Who will stay here to serve the Lord?
Who will stay right here
And serve the Lord from their home?"

Julie C. Gilbert

Others answered in just this way:
"I will stay here to serve the Lord.
I will stay right here
And serve the Lord where need may rise."

Challenge: Now, consider where you are:
Will you answer the call of the Lord?
Whether you stay or go far away,
Serve the Lord with all your heart!"

13. Arms of the Lord

This world may seem cold and cruel.
Do not despair. There's still good here.
Everything touched by God's hand
Shines with His glory.
When trouble comes your way
Step into His loving arms.
Trust me.
You are better off in the arms of the Lord.
You are better off in the arms of the One
Who loved you so much He died
While you were still the enemy.

Now, sometimes people die for their friends,
But few and far between
And none who were perfect,
Save our Lord Christ,
Willingly sacrificed for the enemy.
His arms are always open.
Wait not for tragedy to receive comfort.
Trust me.
You are better off in the arms of the Lord.
You are better off in the arms of the One
Who loved you so much He died
While you were still the enemy.

Julie C. Gilbert

14. Alive in Him

Welcome to life in Christ.
Sit back and hold on tight.
It'll be quite a ride.
You'll have your ups and downs,
But as you wait for pending doom,
Let the sweet scent of a rose
Carry you far away.
Now you know you're alive.
Hallelujah, praise the Lord,
You're alive in Him!

Hear the wind move through the leaves.
Feel its soft kiss touch your face
And take a deep breath.
Now you know you're alive.
Hallelujah, praise the Lord,
You're alive in Him!

Cast your gaze upon the ocean.
Can you see its end?
So shall you never see the end
Of God's love for you.
Now you know you're alive.
Hallelujah, praise the Lord,
You're alive in Him!

15. Follow Him

God doesn't need me, but He wants me,
As He want you, as He want us to follow Him.
So, let us follow Him.
To walk by faith is no easy task,
But we'll make it through.
He will give us strength,
And we will walk on.
So, let us follow Him.
One step in the right direction.
One step is all it takes
To start us on the right path.
We will live our lives to serve the Lord our God,
And He will lift us up.
So, let us follow Him.
God doesn't need us, but He wants us
To follow Him each and every day.
So, let us pray.
For to walk by faith is no easy task,
But we'll make it through.
He will give us strength,
And we will walk on.
So, let us follow Him.

16. Battle for You

Do you feel them watching you,
Guiding your every step,
Telling you right from wrong
That doesn't line up with
Something deep in your soul?
I can see them whisper in your ears.
There's a battle on and it's for you.
The deceiver's lies are so lovely
His promise so sweet.
It's a web of lies meant
To drag you down.
Do not worry.
There's a battle on, and it's for you.
Christ came and won the victory.
You have only to claim new life.

17. Captive to Indifference

Do you understand the times?
Do you understand that we are
Captives to a culture of indifference?
We can see the problems,
And we feel helpless to help.
A thousand thoughts stand in the way
Not the least being:
Your problems are not my problems.
We offer meaningless words like
"Sorry for you pain
Wish I could help, but I can't.
So, have a nice day."
What does that mean to the hurting heart?
If you can't find proper words,
Just hold your tongue and listen well.
The truth may be you can't do a thing.
But you can change your heart,
Offer a prayer, release your chains,
And quit bcing a captivc to this
Culture of indifference.

Julie C. Gilbert

18. Why Do We Cry?

Tell me why, o why, why do we cry?
Why do we live and suffer, only to die?

Why does it rain?
And why is there pain?
Why does the wind blow so fast?
And why is my life racing past?

People are dying all around.
Nowhere is there peace to be found.

I'll tell you why, o why, why we do cry.
Why we live, suffer, and die.

Once upon a time, nothing was wrong,
Then this crafty snake came along.
The first man and woman did sin,
And it seemed as if Satan did win.
But God had mercy on the lost human race.
So, He sent his Son to die in our place.

So why, o why, do we still cry?
Why do we suffer and die?
I can tell you why.

The cause of all our pains
Is that evil still reigns.
This is why we cry.
This is why we suffer and die.

I tell you do not despair

Just Like You

Over the fact that life's not fair.
One day things will be set right.
We'll join hands in Heaven, much to our delight.

Come, join us, one and all
Let God change you from "Saul" to "Paul."
Accept the free gift,
And your burdens God will lift.

19. The City

You and I, we're on a journey
Walking to a city far away,
Beautiful, bright, and clean always.
Pure gold lines the streets.
Joy's common as dust here.
Night and day mean nothing there.
Hearts are light and fixed upon
The Holy One who fills the air.
Let us praise Sovereign God!

Sounds nice.
There's just one thing:
A high wall surrounds that place,
And there's only one gate.
No siege can succeed.
No man can storm that gate
Nor buy entrance with money
Or earn his way by good deeds.
Never fear, there's a way:
Jesus Christ mans that gate.
You're paid in full, walk on through.
The gate lies open to all who
With childlike hearts believe.

20. Steady

What responsibilities do you and I have
To this place we call home?
The world is warming.
The water is rising.
Our fate could be seen as
Steady as the wind.

Steady as the wind.
Steady as good fortune.
Steady as the moonlight
Shining on the ocean.

By and by there comes a time
With naught to do but cry.
That time may be not too far away,
But for now, there's still time
To change this fate.
What can you and I do
To make our world
Steadier than the wind?

21. Take Time

I know you are busy.
I know you are worried,
But I want you to know you should
Take time to worship,
Take time to pray,
"Lord, please help me through life today."
Take the time just to say,
"God, I love You."

Nothing else could ease your mind
Quite like the peace of God
Flowing through and bidding you
Take time to worship,
Take time to pray,
"God, bless the works of my mind today."
Take the time just to say,
"God, I love You."

Not much in life is a guarantee,
But rest assured, if you trust the Lord,
You're in good hands.
So, take time to worship,
Take time to pray,
"Thank You, Father, for my life today."
Take the time just to say,
"God, I love You."

22. Always

You are always. You are for all days.
Not only Sundays. Not only Mondays.
Not only some days.
You are for always.

Fill our minds. Tune our hearts.
Heal everything wrong
In our heads, in our hearts,
Deep down in our spirits.
O Lord, make us come alive.

You are always. You are for all days.
Not only Wednesdays and Fridays.
Not only Saturdays.
Not only Tuesday, Thursday prayers.
Not only some days. You are for always.
You are always.

O God, give us new life.
Give us fresh hearts and deep love
For this lost and broken world.
Carry our spirits beyond the here and now.
There's a war we cannot see,
And we need your weapons to be free.

You are always. You are for all days.
Not only for weekends and free time.
Not only here and now.
You are for always.
You are always.

23. Christian Life: Not Easy but Worth It

So, you say somebody told you
That the life of a Christian would be easy.
I can tell you right now, they lied.
Maybe they didn't mean it.
Maybe they had a better motive in mind.
But all the same, I still maintain, they lied.

We're prone to anger, fear, and pain.
The only difference is that we have hope
Of a better time and a better place.
For one day God will return,
Then anger, fear, and pain will fade away
Like morning mist when the burning
sun decides to show its face.

Though the life of a Christian won't be easy,
It certainly won't leave you worse off
Then you are right now.
The hope and the peace that come from
Loving God and letting Him love you
Will more than make you ready to face the world.

24. For the Enemy

Today, I pray for the enemy.
For all those who hate my country.
For all those willing to take lives.
For all those who do not believe.
May they come to a saving
Knowledge of the Holy One.
What better testimony could there be
Than to turn somebody who would
Kill for a cause
Into somebody who would die
For the sake of the cross?

These people do not lack fervor,
But their hearts are cold as ice
And they lie in the clutches of the evil one.
He will drag countless to Hell.
It's a very sad thing to see.
I cannot change too much,
But today I pray for the enemy:
"Lord, work Your will in them."

25. Will I Ever …

Will I ever learn to be
Patient at all times?
Sometimes I ask myself,
"Why's life got to be so dang complicated?"

See, I started out singing
Lovely praises to my King,
But it turned into a complaining fest
Where I spent time crying out,
"O God, why shut these doors?
Where do You want me to be?
Where am I headed?
I want so bad to be Yours and Yours alone,
But my heart's prone to pride
And my mind wanders
Far away from Your side."

Father, come and teach me
How to praise You properly.
You are Holy and just
And good all the time.

Will I ever be able to say
All I am and ever shall be
Is ever only truly Yours?

26. God Most High

Wish I knew a thousand languages.
Wish I could speak with my hands.
Wish I could say what's on my heart
Some better way.

Even if I had a thousand days.
Even if I tried a hundred ways.
I'd just begin to describe
God most high!

There are no words
Good enough to describe His majesty.
There are no words
Great enough to encompass His glory.

The highest mountains and the open seas
May dazzle and mystify
These are dim in beauty
When compared to God most high!

He possesses wisdom, power, perfect love.
He is timeless, ageless, matchless.
Nothing can compare or compete
With God most high!

27. Glorious Night

Have you truly experience glorious night?
Hear my tale then decide.

On a cool summer's eve,
I shut my eyes tightly,
Thinking just maybe if I listened hard
I would find glorious night.

Exploring the world with only sound,
I could not help but be amazed
By the sweet sounds that soothed my soul.
I listened to the tiny ones
Sing soft praises and wondered
When I last sang my heart out just like that.

My eyes flew open
And fell upon that lesser light.
Like any good ruler it sometimes
Shines less to let us feast our eyes
Upon the starry hosts.

I cannot help but be amazed
By the matchless beauty seen anew
Each and every glorious night!

28. Puzzle Piece

I am only one tiny piece
In this giant puzzle,
And I don't know where I go,
But I can trust in this:
There is a master plan.
There is a holy plan.
There is a place for me in this world,
And God will show me
Where to go when its time.

Waiting has never been a strong
Point that I could claim.
So, I'll follow my heart,
Trusting in this fact:
There is a master plan.
There is a holy plan.
There is a place for me in this world,
And God will show me
How to act when its time.

I shall never have to truly
Worry for a lack of direction,
For I know this one fact.
I can always trust that:
There is a master plan.
There is a holy plan.
There is a place for me in this world,
And God will show me
What to do when its time.

29. Praise

I want to shout to all the world
That God is Lord over all.
I want to praise His Holy name
With every breath that I take.
For if I could praise the Lord God
With every breath that I take,
Well, then, I would be
The happiest person in all of this Earth.
For the chief end of man
Is to praise the Lord with all of our hearts.

God loves all of us.
He's offered us peace through His own Son.
So, I will praise his holy name.
From dawn 'til dusk and far beyond,
I want to shout for all to hear
That God is Lord over all.
So, won't you join in?
And together we will, for all of time
Praise the Lord our God.

30. Beautiful Sight

It's hard to imagine
The love God has for us.
For when we fear, fail, or fall,
He hears us as we call,
Then wraps us in a peace so perfect
We can only bow our hearts,
Open our mind's eye, and boldly declare,

"You're a beautiful sight.
You make all things all right.
Though this world wants to fall
All to pieces everywhere.
You're a beautiful sight.
You make all things all right.
You're a beautiful sight
To this weary soul."

Come free my heart from angry
Shadows of the past.
They hold me here
To doubt, sin, and shame.
I am ready to move on!
For I know that you are …
You're a beautiful sight!
You make all things all right!
You're a beautiful sight
To this weary soul.

31. Liquid Prayers
(Also included in *Beyond Broken Pencils*)

One week slipped by, then almost two.
Each moment made the pain recede,
But I wanted to cry.
I wanted to cry for the angry man
Who stole so many lives.
I wanted to cry for the people
Who would never see home again.
Wanted to cry for the strangers
Mourning a loved one lost.
Wanted to pour out liquid prayers
For everyone wounded in body, spirit, and soul.

Imagine my dismay when I discovered
Something deep within holds my tears at bay.
Have I seen too much to cry?
Or is there too much to cry for?

Though no tears may come,
My heart will weep.
I will weep for the angry man,
For those who fell that day,
For everyone beyond our help.
I will weep for the strangers
Whose pain may not recede.
I will pour out liquid prayers
To bind wounds of body, spirit, and soul.

32. Believe

I believe …
Good things come to those
Who call upon the Lord.

I believe …
Prayer can set wrongs to right,
Melt hearts of stone,
Bring healing and bind up brokenness.

Do not fear …
What the future holds.
For nothing can keep you captive long
If you believe.

I believe …
When darkness, hardship, and heartache
Try to sink your spirits low,
Turn to the Holy One.
Find love, hope, and peace
These are true treasures.

I believe …
Dreams come true
For those who dream big.

33. Higher Calling

There is no higher calling
Than to praise the Lord God.
There is no higher calling
Than to share this good news:
That Jesus came, lived perfectly,
Suffered, died, and conquered death
So all could be free.

There is no higher calling
But to share this news with all
Who have ears to hear, eyes to see,
Or simply an open heart to believe.

There is no higher calling
Than to cast your cares on God.
There is no higher calling
Than to help someone in need.

Now, you may ask why
All these callings are so high.
It is my estimation that every calling
To serve the Lord, whether by prayer or deed,
Is the highest calling we could receive,
So, let us serve.

34. Life Beyond

Do you ever think about
Life beyond the here and now?
Where will you be?
What will you see?
How will you handle
The problems that come your way?

I will trust the Lord to carry me through
Every trial, hardship, and pain.
If there ever was someone qualified
To hear my tale of woe and let me cry,
It would be the Lord who came to Earth to die.
He lived perfectly yet suffered greatly
All to save the lost like you and me.
Praise the Lord always.

Praise the Lord every day
Under grace we can always say,
"God is here with us!"
Because His promises are always sure,
We can live by faith, prayer, and hope
Knowing the future's in good hands.
Praise the Lord always.

35. Moonlight

I had no second chance.
I was captured with one glance.
Have you seen the moon tonight?
It is a strange and beautiful sight.
Weary drivers beware.
The moon compels one to stare.
Do not look too long
Lest you make a turn all wrong!

It's kind of hard to classify,
But I'm sure going to try.
Wonder how God made that color.
It had to be God and no other.
There is power in that light.
I could look forever and never cease
To be amazed by the beauty.

I could stare all night
With awe and delight.
Would to God all could see
Christ's love as clearly as
I see things by the moonlight!

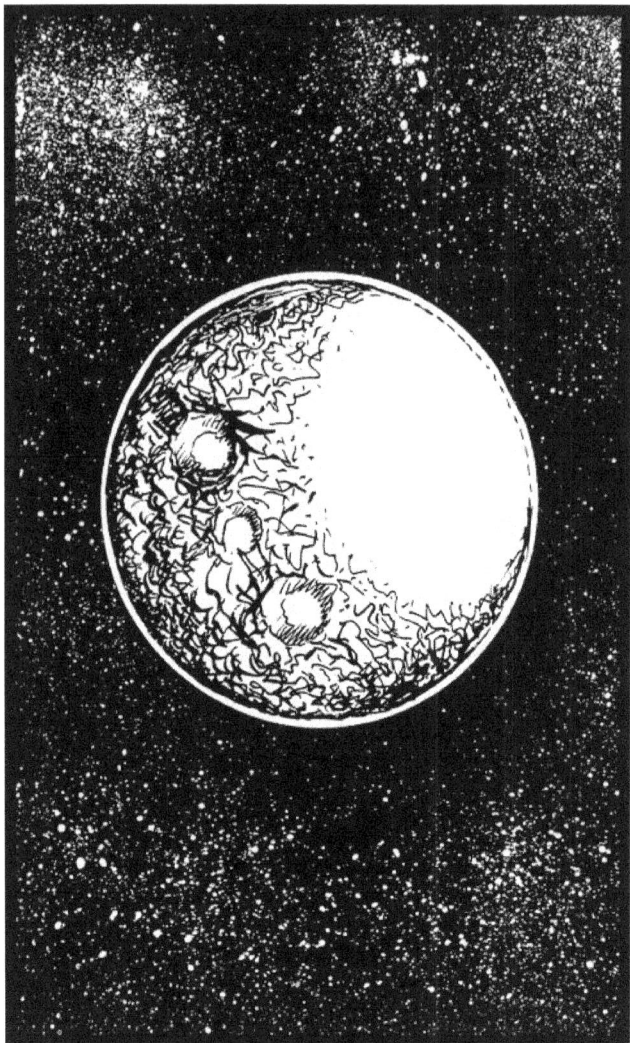

36. No Time Like the Present

There's no time like the present time
To get to know the Lord better.
What keeps my heart away?
Nothing less than a
Thousand little things of life.
And can I change all that?
Of course, I can, I just need to run to Him.

There's no time like the present time
To get to know the Lord better.
How do you keep your best friends?
Why, simply by spending time with them.
God has shown an interest in you.
Why don't you let Him
Love you as only He can?

37. Blood and Renewal

There is blood on my hands.
I know only one way to free them.

God, my God, open my heart,
Take out pride, take out pain.
Leave only mercy, love, and joy.

There is no room for regrets
For peace of mind must be prized
As the highest of riches
One can attain.

Heart, dear heart, feel no fear.
Step forth into dawn.
It is a new day.

There is blood on my hands.
I know only one way to free them.

God, my God, come work in me.
Remove all doubt, sin, and shortcomings.
Leave only You.

38. Grant Me Wisdom

God, grant me wisdom.
God, grant me peace of mind.
It's fair to say I've lost direction
If I ever knew at all.
I wish I had a more eloquent way
To speak my mind and seek Your face.
Yet this simple cry says it all.
God, grant me wisdom.
God, grant me peace of mind.
Uncertainty wants to drown me in self-pity,
But that won't give me answers.
O, I know I'll know at the right time,
Which steps to take and where to go,
Just wish You'd tell me sooner.
I like to think I trust you,
But even as I say aloud:
God, grant me wisdom.
God, grant me peace of mind.
Part of my heart is whispering
May my will be done.
I'll surrender the whispers
For the weight it holds over me
Ought not to be.
I am free in You.

39. Trust the Lord

Where will I be in ten years
And what will I be doing?
Maybe that's too far away.

Where will I be in five years
And what will I be doing?
Maybe that's too far away.

So many choices must be made.
They weigh heavily on me.

I will trust the Lord God
To lead me on the right way.
I will trust the Lord God,
For only He will never fail.

Friends and family and mentors
Of all kinds will fail at times.
Not so with the Lord my God.

On the one hand, I wish
Making decisions was much easier,
But on the other hand,
I'm glad it's hard for me.
It forces me to trust the Lord.

I will trust the Lord God
To lead me on the right way.
I will trust the Lord God,
For only He will never fail.

40. Fingerprint of God

The fingerprint of God
Can be found all around.
In the pattern of a leaf
And the cry of a baby.
In the complexity of a cell
And in the roar of thunder,
There it will be found.

The fingerprint of God
Can be found all around.
In the blaze of the sun
And in the whisper of the ocean.
In the fire of lightning
And the song of the wind,
There it will be found.

The fingerprint of God
Can be found all around.
In the smile of a child
And in the fury of a tornado.
In the dawn of a new day
And the silent slipping away of the old,
There it will be found.

41. Shadowed Smiles

There was a shadow
Over your smile today.
I'm sorry I did not see
It in time to say
I'm sorry to see
There's a shadow
Over your smile today.

I do not know all that goes
On inside your mind,
But you and I both
Know the only One
Who can take your burden,
Make it lighter, and banish
The shadows from your smile.

They may not be able to see
Your point of view.
So, we will pray that one day
The One we know
Will work all this out for good
So we can all see you smile
Without shadows once more.

42. Snow Softly Fall

See the snow softly fall.
Only God could have imagined
Such a peaceful scene.
Almost fear to take a step.
Like it's akin to throwing stones
Through stained glass.

I guess my walk here is all right.
The way the snow falls tonight
This path won't remember me anyway.
I'll turn around, wait a minute,
Watch my footsteps disappear,
Feeling the bitter chill in the air
That reminds me I am so frail.

God come warm me with Your presence.
As I pray and watch the snow softly fall,
I'm reminded of the peace and the
Steep price paid to gain my soul.
Wish the snow would softly fall every day.
Then, I'd always remember my God
Who keeps me warm with His presence.

43. The Truth Remains

I read somewhere today that a
Rich man's money will ransom his life,
But a poor man hears no threats.
Is anyone better off than somebody else?
No way. The struggles may differ,
But they're there all the same.
Life's hard and quite unpredictable.
The flame of life can vanish in a flash
Or flicker uncertainly for years to come.

Eventually, everybody stands
Before the same grand throne,
Answering to the same great God.
Hearing, "Well done, O faithful one."
Or "depart from me, I know you not."
Imagine the sounds resounding around that
throne!
Shouts of joy mixed with much despair.
People crying 'cause Christ died,
And they didn't care.

This picture may be a bit fanciful but
The truth remains:
Your debt is paid,
But the gift's unclaimed.
This choice concerning Jesus Christ
Will shape today, tomorrow, and forever.

44. Prepare

Do you understand the importance of preparing?
You cannot control the things that befall you,
But you can control the way you react to them.
And the key to all this is to lean
on the Lord when times are good.
So that when hard times come,
Leaning on the Lord will be
As natural as breathing,
As natural as seeing,
As natural as hoping to better your life.

45. Hand in Hand

Prayer and praise go hand in hand.
There may be some days
You just don't feel like praising at all.
You can be sure dark days will come.
Days dictated by storms of life.
Days when tears outweigh the smiles.
On such days you need to praise
Stronger, harder, longer.
The more you praise
The higher your heart will soar.

When you heart is weighed down
Prayer can be the cure.
Prayer and praise go hand in hand.
It doesn't matter how well you sing,
So long as it's straight from you soul.
Whether you praise by raising hands,
Bowing your head, or simply closing eyes,
You can be sure God hears.
Always remember prayer and praise
Go so well hand in hand.

46. No Tragedy Quite Like

I read of pain in a far-off place.
Wondered why God let this tragedy strike.
This storm may not touch my shore,
But it sure rocked their shores.
Well, what can I do?
I don't know but I know
There's no tragedy quite like apathy
In the face of tragedy.
Will a prayer really make a difference?
Will money really solve the problems?
In despair, we seek somebody to blame,
Though it's nobody's fault.
Blame can't change this tragedy,
But there's still hope in the Lord.
He can bring you through the pain.
Maybe I can't do much for you,
But you have my prayers every day.
There's no tragedy quite like apathy
In the face of tragedy.
There's no hope quite like hope found in Christ.
It's this hope I wish on you.

47. Stronger than Loss

I cannot say I understand
Exactly what you're feeling.
I feel stunned though I'm on
The edge of this tragedy.

The only mother I ever lost
I never knew,
But I can well imagine the aching loss,
Thinking of how I'd feel in your place.

I can't do much but cling to the cross,
Believing with my heart
What my head already knows:
My God is stronger than loss.

My God pours peace enough to fill the oceans.
When my strength's gone like it so oft is,
I'll hold onto His peace-filled promises,
Knowing my God is stronger than loss.

Let the pain wash through you.
I'll be here to share it.
We can rest in the promise:
Our God is stronger than loss.

48. Only Way to Peace

So, it seems like your whole world
May fall apart around you.
What will you do?
Where will you turn?
Who will you trust in
To carry you through
All of these hard times?

Some may trust in their own selves
To make it through,
And that may work for a time,
But in the end, only those who
Trust in God will be left standing.
Christ is ready. He is willing.
He will hold your hand
And walk you through
Each and every trial.

So, when trouble comes your way
There's not much to say
Except the only way to peace
Is through Jesus Christ's blood.

49. Hope in Loss

Heard you lost your best friend,
And your heart's still hurting.
Heard you're having a tough time
Moving on with life.
I won't claim to know
The depths of such pain,
But I wanted you to hear
Many times in many ways:
You are loved.

There is power in prayer.
There is hope in loss.

Call upon the Great Comforter.
Let Him heal the wounds in your soul.

Love so deep you can feel
Its absence as a void
Can be reclaimed
In sweet memories.
Hold them dear in heart and mind.
Know you are loved.

There is power in prayer.
There is hope in loss.

Peace of mind's not always easy to find,
But it comes from above
And in knowing you are loved.

50. Still Praising

This pain in my mouth in my head
May drive me to silence,
But if I fall silent,
Know that inside I'm still singing.
I'm still praising. I'm still saying,
"You are the best thing in my life!"

This pain in my mouth in my head
May drive me to tears,
But if I start crying,
Know that inside I'm still praising,
For You know all of my pain.
And one day, I'll look back
And remember You were here!

One more day and one more night.
One more moment to reflect.
I'll sing aloud or in my head.
You are God and You are good!
I'll cry out "Praise Your name!"
So the rocks may keep their silence.

51. Powerful Knowledge

My prayers are with you.
I didn't know you had so many problems.
I've been consumed with my own.
Forgive me for the lapse in
Seeing you are hurting.
When you feel weak
Just close your eyes,
Shut out demanding world,
Tune your ear to God,
And let His peace pour over you.

My prayers are with you.
When you're weak then you're strong,
For then you know for sure
You can't make it on you own.
This knowledge is pure power.
Lay still and let tears fall.
They will wash your burdens
And make them ready to be laid bare
To the Holy One, to the only one
Who lift them off your soul.

52. To the Hurting

To the hurting,
I do not know the extent of your pain.
As far as life goes,
You've seen more pain than I have,
And I don't envy you that.
You've seen more anger, more strife,
More heartache than I have,
But I'm asking you to remember this:
There are times when
Humans are a pretty poor representation
Of our Heavenly Father.
Please remember that there are times when
Humans are a pretty poor representation
Of the love and grace shown at the cross
For this lost human race.
Always remember through all of your pain
That God is the perfect one.

To the hurting,
I do not know the extent of your pain,
But I do know that God is a comforter.
Cast yourself in His arms and in the end
You will find the strength to go on …
Even through pain.

53. Worry is a Luxury

When trouble threatens to overthrow your mind,
Remember Job's words.
He'd just found out
Wealth and children and most things
Precious to him were gone,
Yet he had the courage to say:
"The Lord gave, and the Lord has taken away
May the name of the Lord be praised."
Wish I could say the same
If such a lot fell to me,
But I will not worry.
Worry is luxury we cannot
Endure for long with a sound mind.
It tears at sanity one thread at a time.
There is far too much trouble
To go borrowing more.
Take comfort, God knows your breaking point.
Fortify you heart with the Word
Then worry can never conquer you.

54. He Meant You

Yesterday started strangely.
I met Jesus in a dream.
At first, I couldn't understand,
Then, I learned to listen deep inside.

He told me more than could fill one dream.
The pieces I remember
Make me want to know more.

He said life was more than it seemed.
I shouldn't let it slip on by.
Sometimes a good cry and a deep sigh
Are needed to reclaim a sense of calm.

As he turned to walk away,
I called out, "Jesus! Where are you going?"
He said, "I am going to meet a friend.
She is coming home today."

Somehow, I just knew
When he said those words,
He meant you.

The realization released a strange tide:
Joy and sorrow and pain
With a shred of peace at knowing
Our loss was Heaven's gain.

55. Promise

I want to know …
I want to see …
I want to praise …
The God of this universe.

For He is Holy
And He is mighty
And He is perfect
In every way imaginable.

And the best part of all
Is that He loves me
And he died for me
To set me free from all of my sin.

So, now I am His
And for all of time
I will serve
This my God, my Lord, and King.

56. On Limits

There is nothing
Too big or too small
For my God.

He has hung each star out in the sky.
He has seen into the hearts of man.
He has watched over sparrows.
He has clothed fields in flowers.

There is nothing
On Earth or in Heaven or in places unseen
That can't be reached
By my God.

There is nothing
Too big or too small
For my God.

57. Make a Difference

All who are Christian have a hope
Half the world dreams of
And most never find.
Listen carefully to the instructions
Given by God in infinite wisdom.
Then, apply His principles to your life.
So simple to say, yet hard to do!
But God as my witness,
You'll make a difference
If you apply yourself heart, soul, and mind.
Seek out higher things,
Strive for perfection,
Yet fear not to fail.
Love your neighbor,
Care for your brother,
Encourage your sister,
And above all seek God.
He will shine through you
Then, God as my witness,
You'll make a difference!

Just Like You

58. Who Needs Luck?

I want to know the truth.
Sure it might be dangerous,
But I've got to know the truth.
You can wish me luck
Along this perilous path.
But who needs luck when you've got
God on your side?

I want to know the truth.
Whether I live or die lies in God's hands.
So, worry not for me.
If the enemy succeeds in
Separating body and soul
I'll be on my way home.

I want to know the truth.
Truth is worth sacrifice.
With a little bit of luck
The danger will pass swiftly.
But who needs luck
When you've got God on your side?

67

59. Heart of Gold

Some are gifted in the arts.
Some are gifted with hearts of gold.
I know somebody like this.
Most people care for their friends,
But it takes a heart of gold to care
For the downtrodden stranger.
Where'd this heart of gold come from?
I believe everyone has a heart of gold
Buried beneath much selfishness.
Imagine the difference if a few more people
Dug deep down inside, found their
Heart of gold, and acted in love.
It wouldn't be a perfect world,
But some change is better than
No change at all.
Change can be realized by a
Few more people with hearts of gold.

60. Holy Child

What do you think of when
You think of Christmas?
Is it candy; is it gifts?
Is it time spent with your family?
What do you think of when
You think of Christmas?
Is all the stress you get
When thinking of the things to be done?

No matter which side you're on …
There's something neat, there's something sweet
About the notion of our Father God
Coming down to Earth as a little child,
Fully God and fully man,
Tempted in every way, yet always triumphing!

There's something neat, there's something sweet
About the notion of our Holy God
Coming down to Earth as a little child,
Destined to live perfectly,
Destined to be our sacrifice,
Praise God for this Holy child!

No matter what consumes your mind,
Take a moment to reflect upon the
Essence of Christmas:
God's only Son; the greatest gift.
Thank God for this Holy child!

61. Unshakeable

I am not worried,
Merely anxious to know the truth
About a future that lies out of my hands.
There will a time of great joy
When the heart is light
And the eyes dance merrily.
Those days, bright days, will come.
Praise God, they will come.

There will be a time for many tears
When doubt and fear rule the day.
Those days, dark days, will come.
One truth I cling to:
God is unshakeable.

He is Love and He loves me.
I made Him my cornerstone
So sickness, pain, fear, and dread
May turn my world upon its head,
Yet no dark power can steal
The peace in my heart.
It is unshakeable
'Cause it is from God.
I am unshakeable
When I lean on God.

62. Yesterday's Prayer

Did you know that I prayed
For you yesterday?
Well, neither did I, but I prayed that
God would bring comfort to all those
Who are hiding the hurt.
Draw strength from the Lord, my friend,
For no dark time can withstand
The light of His love.

Did you know that I prayed for you yesterday?
Well, neither did I, but I prayed that
God would grant wisdom to all those
Who seek His face.
I know not the hour or the day
A still small voice did declare
"Yesterday's prayers are answered today."

63. Your Eyes Say

Life concerns control your spirit.
I can read as much in your eyes.
They say, "I don't know where I'm going
And that concerns me to the core."
I'd say do not worry if I
Thought it would do any good.
But I can read the rebuttal in your eyes.
They say, "You don't know all my problems.
It's too easy to say don't worry
When you're not in my shoes."

All that is true, far too true.
Maybe the time is just not right
For you to unburden your soul to me,
But I have one suggestion that may
Help you reclaim a sense of peace.
Push all thoughts but the Lord
From your mind for a moment.
You will find Him if you seek Him,
And you will have peace when you find Him.
This holds true forevermore.

64. Sunset

Have you ever stopped
Just to watch the sunset?
It's a beautiful sight!
"Beautiful" only begins to describe
The magnitude of beauty held
In each fading ray as the sun
Seems to say, "Goodbye, until the new day …"
Some may think that sunrise
Out beautifies sunset any day.
I will take their word for that
Because I'm too lazy
To get up that early and check.
Besides, if sunrise is anything
Like its counterpart,
"Breathtakingly beautiful" will only begin to
Describe the glorious dawn of a new day.
Every night God paints the sky
Using every color imaginable.
Truly every sunset is different,
And quite a sight indeed.
If you ever forget "beautiful"
Go watch the sunset.

Julie C. Gilbert

65. Christianese

Anyone ever think that we
Make no sense sometimes?
We say things like
"Bring it to the cross."
And "lay your burdens down."
When all we mean is
"Take your cares to God."

Anyone ever think that we
Make no sense sometimes?
We say things like
"We live in a dark, fallen world,"
And "we are lost without the Lord."
When we mean
"Sin's everywhere, and God saves."

Anyone ever think that we
Make no sense sometimes?
We say things like
"Jesus is the Lamb of God,"
And "Hallelujah, I'm set free!"
Meaning:
"God sent His Son to die for me, and I am happy!"

Why is it easy for Christians
To get stuck on Christianese?
That I could not tell you.
All I can say is that when you do be sure
To give your victim a clue.
For no one likes to be
Stuck lost in Christianese.

66. Praise Anew

I wish I knew some way
To praise You anew each day.
For as each day slips on by
I find myself wondering why
I let myself get all wrapped up
In things that fill my cup,
Yet leave me so empty
When You're the Lord of plenty.

I wish I knew some way
To praise You anew each day.
So, come now, Lord and Father,
Move the rock that is my heart farther
Down along the paths where you hide
Secret treasures for those who can abide.
Give us patience, give us strength.
Give us passion enough to go the length.

I wish I knew some way
To praise You anew each day.
Come, place a song in me,
Then in a short while set it free
To rise and fall.
Teach my heart to heed Your call
To pray and praise with every breath,
Lest I forget the One who gives me rest.

67. Strangest Dream

Awakening from the strangest dream,
I wondered what it could all mean.
I determined to write it down
Until the meaning could be found.
Something told me it would be profound
For its sheer simplicity.

I found myself in a place
Much like this, yet with some trace
Of a dark taint to the morning air.
Imagine my surprise
That upon sunrise
Shadows sprang forth everywhere.

These were no ordinary shadows.
They possessed a nature as cold as gallows
The morning after the doomed has died.
They surrounded strangers
Who knew not the dangers
And assailed their hearts and minds.

As I felt my strength slowly slip away
I knew I needed help without delay.
Words would not come to cry for aid,
Yet answers welled up in my soul:
Only the Lord can keep you whole
In a place where spirits strive.

68. Holy Spirit Fire

Holy Spirit Fire, light us up from inside.
Illuminate the future in our thoughts,
In our hopes, and in our dreams.
Show us all we need to know
To proclaim your truths across the land.
Holy Spirit Fire, light us up from inside.
In the highest halls of power
and in the deepest, darkest pits,
There's a war on for the hearts and souls of men.
Holy Spirit Fire, light us up from inside.
Knit our hearts into one.
We need your heart to understand
The love you hold for every kind of man.
Teach us more of your ways.
Whisper the deep truths into our souls.
Bring us back to life.
Holy Spirit Fire, light us up from inside.
Do not let us trade your glory
For the treasures of this Earth.
Heaven awaits our homecoming
But there is much work to finish here.
Holy Spirit Fire, light us up from inside.

69. Undeserved Cross

It is my hope and fervent prayer
That as you listen to my tale
Some might come to know my Lord.
He's my hope and one true sword.
With Him dwelling deep within
No power can bind me to my sin.

Once upon a time
I led a life sublime
Large family and things aplenty
Still it seemed mighty empty.
Just as I started to despair
I was told of Christ hanging up there
On a cross he did not deserve,
The lives of all to preserve.

At first, I could not comprehend.
What kind of madness would send
An innocent to stand in our stead?
The message was far beyond my head.
Then one day I just knew
What they said had to be true.
The Kingdom belongs to true believers
The truest believers are receivers
Of His freely offered grace,
The one ticket to that place.

Some may say I've had it kind of hard.
I know I am blessed by far.
Just as I started to despair
I remembered Christ hanging up there

Just Like You

On a cross he did not deserve
The lives of all to preserve,
Whether they would call on Him
Or remain content in all their sin.
May it never be said
He stood in vain in your stead.

70. Perfect Rest

There's no magic in words I say.
No power on my own,
But I know the One who holds
The heavens in His hands.
We may never know the reason
Why pain reigns upon the Earth.
Still, we trust in Him.

Father God, Holy Prince,
Take our brokenness.
Take our failures.
Renew our spirits.
Remake our bodies.
Bind our wounds and soothe our souls.
Make us more like You each day.

Grant us courage to call down miracles.
You have brought us out of darkness
To spread hope across this land,
To release your peace everywhere.
Give us patience to face fears and foes.
Let us witness your glory.
May we find perfect rest in You.

71. Sense of Worth

My life like my breath like my mind.
They are gifts from God above
Whose love is matchless.
The more I study how this body works,
The more amazement drives words from my lips.
So is born a sense of worth
Guarded deep in my heart.

I didn't know there were
So many kinds of pain.
Physical, mental, emotional, just to name a few.
The infamous they may say
I don't fit the formula for
Beauty, height, or grace but
Nobody can steal my sense of worth.

Whether you believe or not
God made each person wonderfully unique.
Part of the adventure that is life
Is discovering your gifts.
They can say all they want but
Nobody can steal sense of worth.
It's innate; it's in me and
I'm in God, come what may,
My heart and mind are always safe.

72. Simple Battle Cry

An awakening awaits around the corner.
Can you feel your soul stirring?
There's a darkness creeping in,
But the Light within won't be denied.

When the trials of this world
Try to sink your soul down,
Let your heart sing out:
"Hallelujah! Hallelujah! Hallelujah!"

It's a simple battle cry.
No use wondering why.
Cling to this truth and walk on:
Love will triumph over evil.

Don't you know God wins?
The story finishes in a different age.
But until that day
When the Lord makes all things right,
You can always rest in Him.
Sing: "Hallelujah! Hallelujah!"
Let His peace invade your heart
And your soul will find rest.

73. Awaken

It's been a long time coming,
But at last I see past
The many lies you're telling me.

Why tell me lies with your eyes?
Why tell me you don't care?
Why say it doesn't matter,
When very clearly your heart's
Crying out?

You were meant for
so much more than this.
You were meant for so much more.

Come alive, dear child.
Come alive inside.
Awaken your heart and mind.
You were meant for so much more.

74. Rest in Me

Will you hear my voice
When I call your name?
Will you hear my voice
When I call you?

Will you go, my child?
Will you go?
Will you go where
I send you?

Find peace in this one truth:
No power of man,
No scheme of Hell,
Can take you from my arms.

You are blameless, pure, and holy
When you rest in me.
O, let my love purify.
Let my love renew you.

Your debt, my deed,
It's all done.
Come home and rest in me.

75. Catch the Vision

There's no doubt life's rough
But all those who trust in Christ
Will find true peace.
Once we find peace, let us share.
This is our vision: we will
Love the world, make friends, and pray.
Will you catch this vision? (2X)

Christianity is not hit and run war
It's a revolution.
It may take over your life,
But it sure is worth it!
Would you die for Christ?
Most brave souls would say yes,
But will you catch this vision? (2X)

Will you catch this vision to
Share Christ's love with
All those He died for?
There's a price to pay
And it might be steep at times.
Are you willing to sacrifice to save a life?
Will you catch this vision? (2X)

76. One Family

You may not know who I am,
But if you know the Lord
Then you know who I serve.
And if this is true then you and I
We belong to one family.

We are united in God,
United in Christ, united through the Spirit,
For the three are one.
And since this is true, you and I,
We belong to one family.

You may not know who I am
But one day you will if we both know the Lord.
For the blood of Christ covers us all,
And we will meet one day in Heaven.
And this is true because you and I
We belong to one family.

Now as one family let us serve
All the hopeless that are in this world.
We will serve through our lives;
We will serve through our works,
But most of all let us show them
The love that Christ showed us.
Now that we can hope, we must share
And bring the lost into our family.

77. Moonshine

Last night
We shared something special.
I know you wish you'd shared
That moment with your boyfriend, not best
Friend, and that's all right.
You asked me for my thoughts,
And I could not answer.
I was thinking about the moonshine
Streaming off of your eyes,
And just how crazy he must be
To not see what I see.
If that boy doesn't learn
How to treat a woman
One day, he's going to hurt for it.
If only he'd have been here
Last night.
He'd have seen the moonshine
Coming off of your eyes,
And he'd have never left
Your side.

78. Come Alive

The world says: Worry about today.
Worry about tomorrow.
Store up treasures of the Earth.
Live for the moment.
Fight for yourself
'Cause nobody cares for you like you.

I say: There may be some truths in there,
But they're all wrapped up in lies.
Treasures of Earth fade with time.
Live in the moment,
But fight for your future.
'Cause nobody cares for you like God.

Can you hear His voice?

He says: "Dear child,
I am yours and you are mine.
There's no way to earn my favor.
You have had it since time began.
It's a free gift,
But it still needs to be received.
Let my love transform your life."

Then you will be able to say:
"There is joy, simple joy,
Welling up inside my soul.
There is peace, perfect peace,
Reigning here inside my heart.
There is life, true life.
Flowing freely in me."

Don't you think it's well past time
For you to come alive?

79. Pride and Joy

It's been a long night, a longer day,
And this pain just won't fade away.
Still, I hear my Holy Father speaking to my soul.
He's shouting loud and clear:
"You're my baby.
I love you so much!
You're my pride and joy.
Don't you know my love is infinite?
You'll never have to earn my favor.
I don't love you for what you can do for me.
I don't love you because you love me.
I love for who you are
And who I made you to be.
I made you perfect.
I made you to embody peace.
I made you to reflect my love so clearly
That nobody can deny me.
You're my baby.
You're my pride and joy.
I'm gonna change this whole world
Through the way you carry my Son in your heart.
Just be my baby.
Be my pride and joy.
Rest in my promise that one day
Everything will be all right.
You're my baby.
You're my pride and joy."

80. Standing Still

I am guilty of standing still.
I am guilty of apathy.
I am guilty of perpetuating the idea
That the holy huddle works.

Lord, move me to take a step.
Move me to take two,
For each step I take
Leads to more, and soon,
I'll be running hard for You.

I am guilty of standing still.
I am guilty of pride of heart.
But God is God and Lord of all
And He has the power
To make great things of me.

Lord, please change me from within.
Far too often, I'm standing still
When I should be seizing the day,
And serving God with all my heart.

81. Reflect the One

See the flowers in the fields?
They are marvelous.
Hear the birds singing sweetly?
They are marvelous too.

See the stars twinkling high above?
They are beautiful.
See the moon light up the night?
That is beautiful too.

Watch the sun dance on water?
That is wonderful.
Look at me. Can't you see?
I am wonderful too.

Everything created
Reflects the one and only God.
He was and is and will
Always reign on high.

82. Guiding Light

Father God, Holy One,
Be my guiding light.
Show me what's right.
I know you hear every plea.

Please reveal the hopes and fears
That lie behind tears
Bottled up deep inside
Of those who won't show pain.

I know you see them perfectly.
So be my guiding light.
Show me what's right.
I want to know who burdens you.

Sometimes it seems peace
May be only for dreams.
Wars, fires, and randomness
End life every night.

O Lord, be our guiding light.
Show us what's right.
We know you love perfectly,
So help us cling to you.

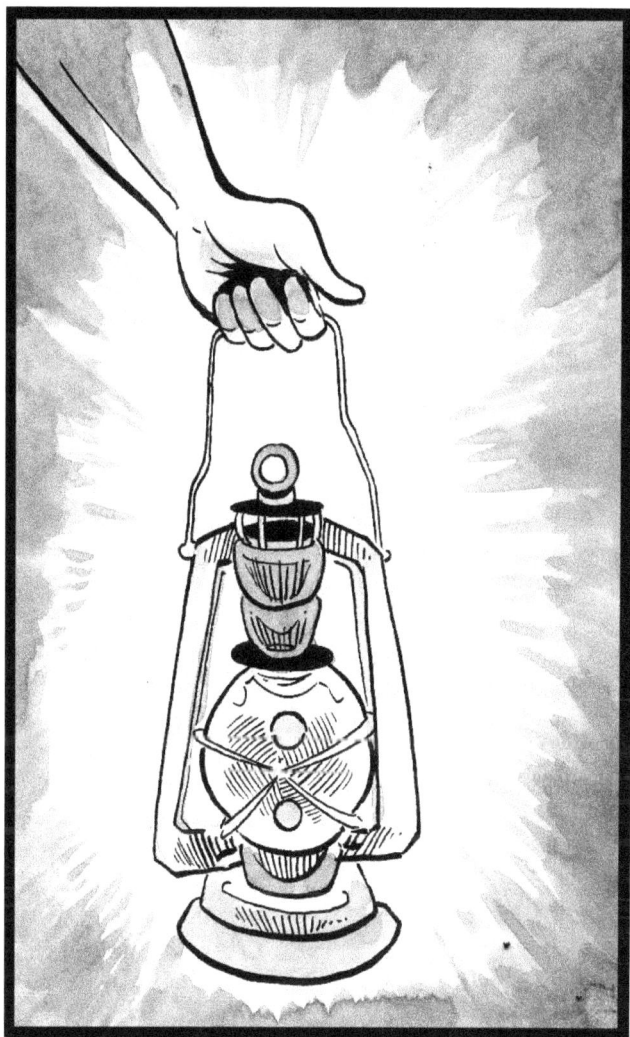

Thank You for Reading:

I hope you enjoyed reading this second Christian Inspirational poetry collection. While reviews are awesome, let's do something different. If something in here touched you in anyway, share it with somebody else.

What does that mean? God has given everybody gifts. If you paint, paint. If you sing, sing. If you draw, draw. If you bake, bake, and so forth. Put the phrase or title or even a whole poem (if applicable) on your labor of love and use it to bless somebody.

It does not have to be shared on social media, and in some cases, it shouldn't. However, if you do, use #MTPchallenge if you choose to share via social media and tag me if you like. I'm on Facebook, Twitter, Instagram, and Mewe.

If you'd like to try some fiction, check out my website (**juliecgilbert.com**). Many stories can be experienced in ebook, paperback, or audiobook.

Hop on the **newsletter** if you want to keep up with life and new release news.
(https://www.subscribepage.com/n7e8l8)

Sincerely,

Julie C. Gilbert

www.ingramcontent.com/pod-product-compliance
Lightning Source LLC
Chambersburg PA
CBHW071818020426
42331CB00007B/1534